o cat

NO GREATER LOVE

MAXIMILIAN KOLBE
NO GREATER LOVE

BONIFACE HANLEY, O.F.M.

AVE MARIA PRESS
Notre Dame, Indiana

#8974354

© 1982 by Ave Maria Press, Notre Dame, Indiana 46556.

All rights reserved. No part of this book may be used or reproduced in any manner whatsoever without written permission, except in the case of reprints in the context of reviews.

International Standard Book Number: 0-87793-257-3

Library of Congress Catalog Card Number: 82-72656

Printed and bound in the United States of America.

Cover and Text design: Elizabeth French

Contents

Kolbe as a prisoner of the Nazis. The depiction is one of a series by the Polish artist, M. Koscielniak.

Preface

On June 7, 1979, Pope John Paul II, the first pope from Poland, a nation that has nurtured Christianity for over a thousand years, walked into the death chamber of Maximilian Kolbe, OFM Conv.

It was not his first visit to this cell in a place known as Birkenau, part of a Nazi complex of concentration camps in Poland called Auschwitz.

"It is well known that I have been here many times. So many times," said the pope. "Many times I have gone down to Maximilian Kolbe's death cell and stopped in front of the execution wall and passed among the ruins of the cremation furnaces. It was impossible for me not to come here as pope.

"I have come here to pray," he said. "Christ wishes that I who have become the successor to Peter should give witness before the whole world to what constitutes the greatness and the misery of contemporary man, to what is his defeat and his victory."

The misery and the defeat was the existence of this complex where the Nazis liquidated 5,000,000 people during World War II. The greatness and the victory was the self-sacrifice of Kolbe, who volunteered for the death chamber to save the life of a condemned man—a husband and father.

"The victory through faith and love was won by him in this place which was built for the negation of faith—faith in God and faith in man," said the pope.

He described Auschwitz as a place of hatred, contempt and cruelty.

"It is impossible to merely visit (this place). It is necessary . . . to think with fear of how far hatred can go, how far man's destruction of man can go, how far cruelty can go. Auschwitz is a testimony of war.

"In this site of the terrible slaughter . . . Father Maximilian voluntarily offered himself for death in the hunger bunker for a brother, and so won a spiritual victory like that of Christ himself."

Kolbe was executed in 1941. Forty-one years later, on October 10, 1982, he would be declared St. Maximilian Kolbe.

His story is a rich one. He came to the concentration camp well prepared. He was a man of deep spirituality, broad vision and seemingly endless energy. Born in the last decade of the 19th century, he died at a time when it seemed the forces of evil had prevailed. He had prepared for and warned against this evil and, through his life and ministry, was very much a part of the 20th century. Pope John Paul II describes him as "the patron of our difficult century."

1 A Circle of Hell

Auschwitz was a circle of hell on the face of the earth. It was a concentration camp where the Nazis, since shortly after their invasion of Poland in September 1939, held political prisoners of all religions and beliefs contrary to their own, along with common and violent criminals.

In Auschwitz cell block 14, on July 30, 1941, prisoners spread the dreaded word: "Someone has escaped." The rumor left the inmates numb with horror, for they knew what was about to happen. At 6 p.m. all the prisoners in the camp were lined up and ordered to stand at attention—absolutely still. The camp commander, Herr Kommandant Fritsch, paced their ranks in silence, scrutinizing them, not telling them what he would do, they knowing what he intended.

It would soon happen. Their Nazi captors would take hostages and a number of men would pay with their lives for the escaped prisoner.

After three harrowing hours of silence and pacing, Kommandant Fritsch told the emaciated wrecks of human beings to break ranks. Soup was brought to the prisoners and a kettle taken to the men in block 14. But they were not allowed to eat. Instead the soup was placed in the cell block, its aroma tormenting the hunger-crazed, exhausted men. Once the prisoners were salivating, the Nazis took the kettle to a nearby field and slowly poured the soup into a drain.

The men would not sleep that night, their

Barbed wire and barracks stand today in silent testimony to the circle of hell on earth known as Auschwitz.

stomachs raw with hunger, their minds frightened by imminent death.

At 6 a.m. the next day, the entire camp was lined up. Fritsch announced, ''The fugitive has not been recovered. Therefore 10 of you must die in the starvation bunker. Next time it will be 20.'' He dismissed all the prisoners except the men from block 14 who were ordered to stand at full attention in the camp yard. The men, weakened by months of imprisonment and inhuman treatment, stood rigidly in the broiling sunlight for several hours without food or water. One by one they fainted. At half past three the guards allowed the unfortunates a bit of rest and gave them some thin soup and water. For 10 prisoners it was their last meal on earth.

As the sun set, the Nazis began the dreadful process of selecting the doomed. An Auschwitz survivor wrote: ''During my two years at Auschwitz, I stood in about a dozen lineups like this. I never really got used to them, but after a while a man just got numb. The worst was when I was standing in the front row. The commander of the camp, in selecting the hostages, pointed at me—so I thought! It was the most frightful moment of suffering I ever lived through. It turned out that he was pointing at the man behind me. These poor hostages were sentenced to starve to death.''

And now, on this warm July evening, Gestapo Kommandant Fritsch was selecting 10 innocent men to die of starvation. Slowly he paced the ranks, stopping suddenly in front of a victim, demanding to inspect his mouth. ''Open your mouth! Show me your teeth! Stick out your tongue!'' It was a pointless inspection added only for drama. His selections for the death chamber were arbitrary, neither the weakest nor the strongest.

He ordered the 10 men to step forward and march to the underground bunker where they would be locked until hunger and thirst claimed them.

Suddenly, Sergeant Francis Gajowniczek, one of Fritsch's choices, burst out in tears. "How I pity my wife and children whom I'm leaving as orphans."

The men of cell block 14 watched the grotesque proceeding with feelings of both horror and relief. They now stood immobile, frozen in fear. All but one. He broke ranks and approached the camp commander and managed to kiss Fritsch's hand.

"What does this Polish swine want?" Fritsch asked the translator.

"I want to die in place of one of the condemned," replied prisoner #16670, Raymond Kolbe.

"Why?" asked the commander in amazement.

Kolbe knew he could not upstage the commander and had to offer a reason that would allow Fritsch to save face. He used the unwritten law of the Nazis, that the sick and weak must be liquidated.

"I am an old man, sir, and good for nothing. My life is no longer of use to anyone."

"In whose place do you wish to die?" asked Fritsch.

"For the one with the wife and children," he said pointing to Sergeant Gajowniczek.

No one ever remembered a prisoner breaking ranks before. Even more amazing was the fact that the guards did not shoot him when he did.

Fritsch scrutinized the inmate standing before

Kolbe confronts his captors.

Entrance way to the starvation bunker in Auschwitz in which Maximilian Kolbe died.

him, a frail man in his forties. The sufferings of concentration camp life and illness had ravaged his body. There was about him, however, a compelling aura of calm and peace. During his career as ruler of this empire of death, Fritsch had seen many things, but never before had he encountered someone willing to give his life for another prisoner.

"Who are you?" the Nazi asked.

"I am a Catholic priest," replied Father Maximilian Kolbe, a Franciscan friar.

A "priest" was all that Fritsch had to know. Priests occupied the second lowest rung of the camp ladder. On the lowest were the Jews. For Fritsch there was no problem as long as he had 10 hostages. And so the kommandant ordered the priest to take Sergeant Gajowniczek's place in the starvation bunker. He was about to honor the ideal he had recalled to his fellow friars only a few days before his arrest, when he said, "The greatest grace of God and the greatest happiness of man is the ability to attest to one's ideal with one's blood."

2 Great Faith, Great Hope, Great Love

Who was this remarkable priest? What is his story? Of what stuff was he made that he could offer his life with such courage on that fateful July night? What caliber of man could lead other men to choose serenity, calmness and faith in place of hatred and despair in the circumstances of a cruel death deliberately provoked by his fellowmen; not a quick death, but a hideous death brought about by willfully withholding food and water?

Perhaps Pope Paul VI, in speaking of Father Kolbe, can best describe our sentiments. The pope, in October 1971, remarked:

> The picture of the ending of this man's life is so horrible and harrowing that we would prefer not to speak about it, not to contemplate it anymore, in order not to see what lengths may be reached by inhuman arrogance. . . , but history cannot forget this frightful page. And so it cannot but fix its horrified gaze on the luminous points that not only reveal but actually overcome its inconceivable darkness.
>
> One of these points, perhaps the one that glows most brightly, is the calm, exalted figure of Maximilian Kolbe. His name will remain among the great. . . .

And so the little priest who is known to the world as Father Maximilian Kolbe, OFM Conv., who desired nothing else than to disappear at death completely into

Father Kolbe as a prisoner in 1940.

God, today is very much alive. The dust of his memory has been charged with light and is gradually suffusing the world. As Christ rose out of the earth to lead us to new hope, so the memory of Father Maximilian Kolbe has risen from the dreaded bunker at Auschwitz to remind us that the work of Christ continues.

Father Maximilian's death, with the intense generosity and Christian love that characterized it, was only the final act of a life filled with great hope, great love and, above all, great faith.

He was born on January 8, 1894, in the village of Zdunski Wola, Poland, a village of weavers near Lodz. His parents, Julius and Maria, named him Raymond and had him baptized in the parish church of the Assumption of Our Lady. He was the second of three sons that lived, the oldest being Francis, the youngest, Joseph. Two other sons died in childhood.

Tragedy marked the lives of many of the Kolbes. The father, Julius, was a Polish patriot living in an area of Poland that had been under Russian rule for 100 years. He was active in free Polish causes and inspired in his sons a love of their native land. In 1914, World War I broke out, and Julius, whose sons were all now studying with the Franciscans, joined the Polish army. He fought the Russians on the eastern front and was captured. In one of those strange twists of fate he was carrying a Russian passport since he came from Russian-occupied Poland. Finding the passport, the Russians hanged Julius Kolbe as a traitor.

Francis, like both Raymond and Joseph, joined the Franciscans where he took the community name of Alphonse. During World War I he took leave of absence from the religious order and joined the liberation movement where he served as an intelligence officer and was wounded.

Nearly 25 years later he would answer the same call and again become a Polish intelligence agent, this time to resist Hitler and the Germans. In 1943 he was captured by the Gestapo and was shipped to Auschwitz, where he evidently died only a few years after his brother's heroic death there.

Mrs. Kolbe was an industrious woman who helped support the family by working as a nurse and midwife, and by running a secondhand store. With her children on their own and her husband dead, she took up residence with a convent of Felician sisters in Cracow where she lived out her years.

As a youngster, Raymond was charged with energy, and was quickly turning his mother's hair gray. Punishment for his pranks and escapades was common enough, especially for a 13-year-old, but one day after a vigorous spanking, Mrs. Kolbe asked her son, "Raymie, what will become of you?"

The mother's exasperated question evidently triggered something within the boy. He suddenly became more serious-minded and obedient at home and began to spend more time in prayer. His mother, delighted, puzzled and worried all at the same time, as most mothers would be with such a change, did not quite know how to handle it. Finally Mrs. Kolbe asked Raymie just what was going on. The little boy responded: "After you asked me what would become of me, I prayed to the Blessed Mother and asked her what will become of me.''

The little boy then said that the Blessed Mother offered him two crowns, a white one and a red one. ''She asked me which one of these crowns I wanted,'' little Raymond explained, ''the white one signifying that I will persevere in purity and the red one that I will be a martyr. I told Mary that I wanted them both.''

We can only imagine how Mrs. Kolbe felt after that conversation.

Father Kolbe's mother,
Maria, in 1941.

In later years, after his death, his mother related the episode. "What convinced me that my boy was telling the truth," she explained, "was his radical transformation. From that day on, he was not the same as before, and often he would come to me with a radiant face to speak about his future martyrdom, as though this were his most cherished ambition. And I prepared myself for it, just as Our Lady did after she heard Simeon's prophecy."

In 1907, when he was 13, Raymie entered the Franciscan minor seminary in Lwow. Seminary professors were delighted with his intelligence, his talent for mathematics and physics, and predicted great things for Kolbe. As a teenager, his vision was deep and his horizons extremely broad.

At this point Raymond had not definitely decided to become a Franciscan friar. He appreciated his own inventive talents. Totally absorbed in love of his country, he felt he might best serve Poland as a military officer. Now approaching his 16th year, Kolbe would soon have to decide which path of life to follow.

It was a painful decision to make, but finally in 1910, Raymond Kolbe entered the Franciscan Order and received his new name, Maximilian. The following year he professed his temporary vows and was sent to Cracow to study. There his teachers and superiors recognized his ability and in 1912 sent him to Rome to study at the Gregorian and the International Seraphic College. He studied theology and philosophy and earned doctorates in both.

The Eternal City's cosmopolitan atmosphere broke open the provincial mold of the young Pole. He

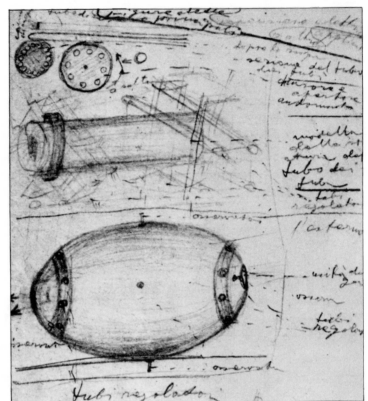

While a student in Rome, Father Kolbe developed an interest in space travel and sketched this design for a rocket.

Father Kolbe wrote an article in Italian on space travel and submitted it to a scientific journal. The journal did not use it since it was only interested in articles on actual inventions rather than hypothetical projects.

realized that there were men and women suffering because of the evil that pervaded so much of the Western world. He found, too, that there were people who had never heard of Christ, or cared very much about him.

Something else happened to Raymond in Rome. He became very deeply interested in the Blessed Mother's role in the work of salvation. He applied his enormous intelligence to a struggle to comprehend Mary and her meaning. Indeed he questioned whether Mary had any vital role to play in healing and in rescuing the human race from evil and its horrifying effects on individuals and society. Was Mary simply the sweet and delightful mother who really had a secondary position as far as the happiness and eternal destiny of humanity were concerned?

This area of theology totally absorbed Friar Maximilian. The mystery of Mary eventually would dominate his whole life. Already he began to perceive God's mother as the divinely chosen agent through whom the tide of darkness gradually and inexorably gathering about the 20th-century world could be reversed. The friar now dedicated himself to her service and, because of his military cast of mind, dubbed himself her knight. For the first time, as far as we know, he began to think of himself as the knight of Mary, the Immaculate Mother.

Stirred by an interior vision that saw Mary as Queen of the Universe, Maximilian began to express outwardly his deep conviction of Mary's role in human society. He wrote:

> This is the age of the Blessed Virgin; now begins the
> era of Mary Immaculate. Mary is the Mother, the
> real Mother, of each one of us . . . and the Queen of
> Society. We must practically recognize Mary's mis-
> sion as Queen and Mother, then let her act fully,
> freely; she will then have unheard-of triumphs; she
> will conquer every enemy.

His keen intelligence perceived the signs of the times.
The forces of evil were gathering, the fist of war form-
ing. It would drop quickly on the world in two
sledgehammer blows—World War I and World War
II.

Maximilian's adult life was framed by these two
horrible events. And yet, as this tide of evil ebbed and
flowed over our world and convulsed it in pain and in-
describable agony, Maximilian never ceased to believe
that the power of God was still at work. With all his
heart, he felt that, through Mary, Christ was continu-
ing his saving work for the human race and that the
healing of society through the Immaculate Mother was
becoming more and more a reality. Before his ordination in Rome, in April 1918, the young Franciscan,
with the approval of his superiors, organized a group of
friars into what he called "The Knights of Mary Immaculate."

This little group, reminiscent of Francis of Assisi's
Knights of the Round Table, dedicated themselves to
win for Mary, by word, example and prayer, nothing
less than the whole world. Their first meeting took
place the evening of October 16, 1917. It was just a
year before the end of World War I.

*The newly ordained
Kolbe in 1919.*

3 Beginnings at Grodno

Following his ordination, Father Kolbe returned to Poland and was assigned to the Franciscan Seminary in Cracow. There he taught philosophy and church history, and continued his work as a Knight of Mary.

He immediately began to organize "focus groups" of the Knights among his confreres. Later the young professor gathered about him people, religious and lay, devoted to Mary. With the permission, encouragement and blessing of Bishop Adam Sapieha of Cracow, he organized them into what he called the "M.I.," the Militia of the Immaculate. The objective of this Militia was the same as that of the Knights of Mary Immaculate he had established while in Rome: to conquer the whole world for Mary. He took an unusual approach in that he did not want to have an organization. Maximilian stressed the notion of the Militia being a movement, not encumbered by strict organizational forms and bylaws. It would be nurtured simply by the idea that the world could be won over for Mary through prayer, example and the word.

"Let us permeate everything," he wrote, "and cure all ills with its healthy spirit; let us spread out for the greater glory of God through the Immaculate and for the good of mankind."

At first the movement attracted only the young and the intelligentsia, but Father Kolbe was sensitive to technology's potential and began to make plans to reach the masses through the press and radio. He saw the new and marvelous discoveries as vehicles for bringing the message of Mary and her role in the healing of the broken human race to the knowledge and the hearts of the people. No dreamer, Father Kolbe, in January 1922, instituted a monthly magazine called *The Knight of the Immaculate*. During the '20s and early '30s, many magazines appeared throughout the Catholic world, but few entered the publishing field surrounded with the absolute poverty of *The Knight*. No "knight" ever went into combat so ill-equipped. Maximilian had no financial backing, could not even secure a loan, and Poland at the time was gripped in a fierce financial depression. His Franciscan colleagues gave him little support or comfort. They felt the magazine would die in infancy. His superiors, somewhat reluctantly, permitted the new project, despite the depressing times. Father Kolbe, to everyone's amazement, managed to keep afloat financially.

From his student days in Rome, when he contracted tuberculosis, deplorable health plagued Maximilian. So sickly was he upon his return to Poland after his ordination that Kolbe's superiors felt he would live no more than a few months. Even at this stage of his career, illness caused difficulty in his breathing and slowed his pace. He experienced frequent hemorrhaging. Witless confreres dubbed him "Marmalade" because of the slowness of his movements.

Friars of the Cracow monastery dedicated themselves to the traditional works of hearing confessions, preaching, saying Mass, attending the sick and so forth. When Father Kolbe, a relatively young priest, arrived with his impractical dream of publishing a seemingly meaningless magazine, he hardly fit into their orderly scheme. Although Maximilian was a devoted religious and fulfilled the common prayer life conscientiously, the ceaseless activity, the accompanying bustle, and the business of the press upset the Cracow friary.

The friars were too well aware that Kolbe had initiated the magazine only after obtaining the superiors' reluctant permission. He went into debt to purchase supplies and mailing equipment for his first issue. For people today who spend most of their lives in debt, it is difficult to realize that for a European friar this was a *Father Kolbe at work in his publishing office.*

frightful condition. When Maximilian, then, went into debt and could not find money to pay it off, his provincial superiors had no means to help him.

In effect, they said, "We did not ask you to start this, and we are not going to bail you out." The provincial and the friars of Kolbe's Cracow community looked upon the whole situation as the zeal of a young priest outrunning his common sense.

But, as always, God uses saints to prove that his ways are not human ways. Two sources came to Maximilian's assistance in his first financial crisis. A parish priest in Cracow, moved by the simplicity and purpose of Maximilian's work, donated most generously and unexpectedly toward the magazine. This helped pay a good part of the debt, but still the priest-publisher needed more to finally pay it off.

With nowhere to turn, Kolbe knelt before the Blessed Mother's altar at St. Francis Basilica in Cracow. During his prayers the young priest became oblivious to everything; and then, as he concluded, he rose and noticed on Mary's altar a small envelope. He went to the altar, picked up the envelope, and saw written on it, "For you, O Immaculate Mother." Maximilian opened the envelope and found in it the exact sum that he owed his creditors.

Business conditions, however, did not improve in Poland. Five times during the first year, Maximilian changed printers to meet continually rising prices. It was not long before he decided to organize his own printshop. In October 1922, the provincial authorities transferred him to Grodno, on Poland's eastern border, where there was more room for him to expand.

Here, things improved greatly for him and his work. The provincial assigned a brother to help him, and between Father Kolbe and Brother Albert, a deep bond of friendship grew as together they pioneered their little magazine. Another brother and a candidate were assigned to him, and in 1925 other candidates for the order began to join him.

Because of the financial depression, Father Maximilian still had difficulty gathering funds. One evening an American Franciscan provincial joined the friary recreation at Grodno. Maximilian's companions were poking fun at him for fund-raising in these hard times. The American provincial listened. The American's temper flared slightly, and he chided his Franciscan brethren: ''You ought to help this man instead of ridiculing him.'' To back up his words, the provincial made a generous donation to Maximilian's press. It was one of the best foreign-aid investments ever made.

Despite the fact of the bad Polish economy, Father Kolbe quickly gathered enough funds to purchase the press. Another friar joined his editorial staff. The three Franciscans now set to work writing, setting type, printing, and distributing the 5,000 copies of *The Knight.*

Besides all this work, Father Kolbe was assigned to parish duties at Grodno. Not a physically strong man, he accepted these extra and seemingly unfair burdens without complaint. He fulfilled them enthusiastically. His two companions also had friary assignments and Kolbe insisted that they fulfill them. Thus it was not unusual for the three of them to work by day in the friary and parish, and all night long on the magazine.

Circulation of *The Knight* increased by leaps and bounds. Maximilian now had to purchase a Linotype machine for setting type. Not one of the friars publishing *The Knight* knew the first thing about a Linotype. Maximilian's confreres, judging the purchase of the expensive machine as another folly, showered a small storm of ridicule on the poor friar. But they forgot for whom the young priest was working. It was Mary, and she soon showed her appreciation. Immediately after the Linotype's arrival, a young

Brothers setting type for Father Kolbe's magazine.

mechanic knocked on the friary door at Grodno and asked admittance to the order. The youth was a highly trained specialist and soon had the Linotype humming away happily, pounding out type for Maximilian's publication.

More and more brothers came to join the publishing enterprise, and soon the group formed a community within the Franciscan community at Grodno. Production of the little magazine within three of the worst depression years in Poland soared from 5,000 to 45,000 copies per issue. In five years it reached 60,000, while the Militia of the Immaculate numbered 125,000 members.

The strain, however, proved too much for Kolbe, and once more tuberculosis struck and forced him into a sanitarium.

Maximilian must now have suffered some deep sense of frustration. His work was just beginning to bear fruit. His Militia was now paying for itself. His work of teaching about the Blessed Mother and promoting Marian devotion through the magazine was proceeding very effectively. But now he was ill. Realizing he could now best serve through his suffering, Kolbe accepted the illness with his profound sense of calmness and patience. Doctors released him after some months in the sanitarium, and he returned to pursue a new and bold project.

4 The City of the Immaculate

In 1927, with the circulation of *The Knight* at 70,000, Father Maximilian had to find a new location for his publishing enterprise. The priest discovered a large property, a forest near Warsaw, belonging to a Polish prince, Jan Drucki-Lubecki. Moved by the religious spirit of Maximilian and the purposes of his work, the prince generously gave the property to the Franciscans.

Maximilian moved the friars and their equipment to this new location in October 1927. Cutting the forest's raw timber, the friars constructed a chapel, sleeping quarters, equipment huts, workshops and administrative offices. These early pioneering days were very trying. The Polish winter came early and was severe. But the friars were strong men, and adversity brought out the best in them. Their dedication to their work and its purpose forged a tremendous bond of love, joy and cheer between Maximilian and these other sons of St. Francis.

By now tuberculosis had destroyed a portion of Kolbe's lungs. Although he hemorrhaged frequently, he would permit himself no privileges but indeed led in the energetic prosecution of this work.

Wise men must have shaken their heads when they saw the ragged little group of men building their dream in the cold forest outside the gates of Warsaw. What brought them together, what kept them working, what

Father Kolbe, with glasses, chats with Prince Drucki-Lubecki, the benefactor who provided the land for Niepokalanow.

developed among them in the midst of so many contrary currents, can only be explained as the movement of God's grace in this forgotten corner of the world.

Incredible things happened in that forest of the Polish prince. Building by building, the City of the Immaculate, as the friars called this place, grew. The original community of two priests and 18 lay brothers and candidates who arrived in 1927 grew within a decade to 650 conventual friars and candidates, and 122 minor seminarians. Thirteen of these friars were priests. The area, known as Niepokalanow, eventually boasted the largest religious community of Franciscan men in the world.

For a number of reasons the work of building the City of the Immaculate was done entirely by the brothers. First, there was money, or the lack of it. Whatever contributions and support he had, Father Kolbe put back into his communications projects, mostly to buy more printing equipment.

More importantly, there was Father Kolbe's love of Franciscan poverty. He wrote:

> I could do religious work in other communities like the Jesuits or Dominicans, but the Franciscan concept of poverty was more attractive to me. I am most happy to be a Franciscan and work on the foundation of Franciscan poverty.
>
> If in our work, poverty is neglected, the whole work will disintegrate.

He believed that nothing was too poor, nothing was too good in the service of God and the Immaculate. He

Pages 37-39:
Scenes from the City of
the Immaculate in the
1930s.

never asked for special food or consideration because of his poor health, never had clothes better than those of his brothers, nor money for his own use.

As the first decade passed, building after building grew from the forest floor. During the first five years they constructed a chapel, a college, a novitiate, a friary for professed Franciscans, a 100-bed hospital, an electric plant and formed a fire department.

This external growth was only a reflection of the personal development and growth in the spirit of the friars under Maximilian's direction. He realized that this tremendous burst of energy could produce wealth, and this, he knew, would destroy his friars and their work. Any hint of financial profit repelled him. He made it clear that if the friars ever worked for any other aim than the service of Mary, he would separate himself from their work.

On the eve of the outbreak of World War II, almost 17 years after Maximilian had started *The Knight,* its circulation had jumped to 750,000. His daily paper, *The Little Journal,* had a circulation of 137,000 with double that on Sundays. Besides these, his presses were offering no less than eight different publications varying from a spiritual journal in Latin for priests to youth magazines to an illustrated periodical called *The Sporting Journal.* In addition, the M. I. Press published a variety of books and pamphlets.

But the little priest kept his success in perspective. "All progress is spiritual," he taught, "or it is not progress." The foundation of the City of the Immaculate rested on the holiness of the life of the Franciscans gathered there. With discerning simplicity,

Father Kolbe made clear the only formula for their success: "We ourselves must first be holy."

The spirituality of Father Kolbe centered on the Eucharist and on Mary. He saw his work and that of the friars as a form of adoration of the Eucharist. He believed that devotion to the Immaculate leads to devotion to the Eucharist, which perpetuates the real presence of Christ in the church.

On devotion to Mary he wrote:

One gives himself to Mary in a perfect manner by giving himself to her as her thing and her property. From that moment, the first condition in order to belong entirely to her is the total offering of oneself to the Immaculate.

He also wrote that:

The most perfect love of a creature for God is found in the Immaculate, the creature without blemish of sin, whose will had never been, even for an instant, separated from the will of God.

We wish to do the will of the Immaculate, to be perfect instruments in her hands, be totally guided by her, in perfect obedience.

But his Marian devotion was much more than simply a cult of the Blessed Mother. He believed that the best way to love Jesus was through his mother, and the best way to love the Father was through Jesus. By loving Mary we love God and can identify with him; in living in Mary we live in Jesus and become one with him.

He wrote that "those who give themselves to the

Immaculate will not be lost; moreover, the more they
belong to her, the more they belong to Jesus and to the
heavenly Father.''

This love of Jesus and the Father through devotion
to the Immaculate was consistent with the history and
tradition of the Franciscans. He wrote:

> Beginning with St. Francis and St. Bonaventure, our
> order always honored her with this title (Immaculate
> Conception). Later on Duns Scotus and the Fran-
> ciscan school defended this precious privilege of hers
> until the solemn definition of the dogma of the Im-
> maculate Conception. This continuity is like a golden
> thread in our order, and, perhaps we can say, a
> beginning of the renewal of a demoralized society,
> for it was said of her: ''She shall crush your head
> . . .'' (Gn 3, 15) and ''You alone have destroyed all
> heresies in the whole world.'' Let us often plead in
> the words of Duns Scotus, ''Let me praise you, most
> holy virgin; give me strength against your enemies.''

Prior to World War II and the holocaust that would
engulf Europe and claim him as a victim, Maximilian
wrote:

> Modern times are dominated by Satan and will be
> more so in the future. The conflict with hell cannot
> be engaged by men, even the most clever. The Im-
> maculate alone has from God the promise of victory
> over Satan. She seeks souls that will consecrate
> themselves entirely to her, that will become in her
> hands forceful instruments for the defeat of Satan
> and the spread of God's kingdom.

An overview of Niepokalanow from its main entrance. Picture was taken in the mid-thirties.

Scene from the chapel at Niepokalanow. By 1937 it was the largest community of Franciscan men in the world.

*Enjoying the company
of some students in
1939. The Nazis were
about to invade
Poland.*

*Father Maximilian
visiting the minor
seminarians on an
outing in 1937.*

For Father Kolbe, obedience was a key virtue in the struggle with evil. "Our only task is to fulfill the will of God through perfect obedience," he would often tell the friars at Niepokalanow. He taught that the will of the Immaculate was united with the will of God, and that her followers should unite their will with hers. The Knights of the Immaculate were practicing the perfection of the virtue of obedience.

> But this does not mean that we should have no initiative. On the contrary we ought to openly manifest our heartfelt thoughts and desires to our superiors, provided we are also ready to accept the decision of obedience, even if it is not our personal desire.

"The true Niepokalanow," he explained, "is in our hearts. Everything else is only secondary." A dialogue between Father Kolbe and one of his confreres has survived the years. It echoes the famous conversation between Francis and Brother Leo.

"Tell us, Father, in what does true progress in our work consist?" the brother questioned the superior.

"It is in being poor, without our own resources," Father Kolbe replied.

In lyrical phrases that 20th-century followers of St. Francis can well understand, Father Kolbe goes on: "If we were to have the latest machines, if we were to use all technical improvements and all discoveries of modern science, this would not yet be true progress. If our magazines doubled and even tripled their circulation, that would not be true progress."

"What, then, is necessary, Father," the brother

asked, "to have true progress here in our work?"

Without hesitation, the priest answered: "Our exterior activity, whether in the friary or outside it, does not constitute Niepokalanow. Even if all members of the Militia abandon us, even if all our magazine circulation went to nothing, even if all this plant were dispersed like leaves struck by the autumn wind; if, despite all these things, the ideal of love and service of God and his Blessed Mother were to grow in our hearts, then, my little children, we can say we are in full progress."

Thus Maximilian established priorities for his friars. Prayer came before work. Despite the stupendous activity of the city, he insisted that the friars spend three and a half hours each day in community prayer and meditation. The friars together shared the common life; there was no distinction between priest and brother. The only exception to the common poverty was those who were ill. Father Kolbe showered upon the sick the best of food and medicines.

5 Mission to Japan

Kolbe's story now takes an incredible turn. One day, when riding a train, Father Maximilian met some young Japanese students. He was moved by their kindliness and courtesy. His heart was broken to know that these fine young people were deprived of the knowledge of Christ and his gospel. Characteristically, he felt he had to do something. Thus Maximilian approached his superiors to seek permission to establish a City of the Immaculate in Japan.

From anybody else the idea would have been bizarre. After two decades, however, Father Kolbe's superiors had learned to expect anything of him.

Thus in February 1930, along with four brothers, Maximilian left the City of the Immaculate in Poland to establish another such community in far-off Japan. With characteristic humility Maximilian slipped quietly out of Poland. He took leave of neither his brother, a Franciscan priest, nor his mother, who by now was with the sisters in Cracow. In the tenderness of his own heart he could not bear such farewells. He wrote later from Japan to his mother: "You will forgive me, Mother, for not calling on you before going on my journey."

As the little group made its way through Europe to the port of Marseilles, France, Maximilian stopped at Lisieux, the burial place of St. Therese. He also visited Lourdes.

The missionary spirit of Therese of Lisieux who,

Father Maximilian, center, on his way to Japan in 1930 with four brothers from his community. The picture was possibly taken in Hong Kong.

from her hidden cell, prayed to conquer the whole world, appealed to Maximilian's belief that the life of prayer and personal holiness had to be the basis for any work for Christ and his mother.

On his way to Japan he also stopped at Saigon, Hong Kong, Shanghai and Tokyo, hoping that he could eventually establish a City of the Immaculate in each of these Asian cities.

On April 24, 1930, the little band of friars arrived at Nagasaki, the city that had been Japan's window on the world during its centuries of isolation, and the city in which Christianity had survived nearly 300 years of persecution. The Japanese bishop, delighted with Father Maximilian's plans, offered his support immediately. In return, the prelate requested that the priest teach philosophy and theology in the Nagasaki seminary. Father Maximilian joyfully acceded and the first steps toward building a Japanese City of the Immaculate were taken.

These Polish friars were either full of madness or full of faith. About to publish a magazine in Japanese, they could neither read, write, nor speak Japanese. They knew nothing of Japanese law, culture, labor practices, or machinery. In short, they knew nothing of Japan. Yet, incredibly, within one month, Father Maximilian and his group published and distributed their first Japanese issue of *The Knight*.

The minor miracle was the work of many hands and minds. A Japanese Methodist translated Italian and English articles into Japanese, and a Japanese university professor translated articles from German into Japanese for this first issue. Father Maximilian

Father Kolbe in Japan meets with monks from a Buddhist monastery.

The Franciscan church in Nagasaki that was part of the Garden of the Immaculate that Father Kolbe established. The church survived the atomic bomb that nearly destroyed the city.

wrote articles in Latin, and a Japanese seminarian translated the Latin into Japanese. Thus final articles often went from Polish to Latin to Japanese.

To further comprehend the impossible task these men accomplished it is necessary to realize that it was absolutely contrary to Japanese custom and etiquette to seek subscriptions through the mail. Thus the friars advertised *The Knight* in trains, streets, and other public places. Interested Japanese would send a postcard with their address. Only on receipt of that card could the friars solicit a subscription to their magazine.

The very simplicity and courage of these friars attracted both Christian and non-Christian Japanese. Vocations began to come to the Franciscans from the people around them. Within four years the little community of five had grown to 24 friars. Maximilian soon established a minor seminary and within six years there were some 20 Japanese studying for the priesthood in the Franciscan Order.

The Franciscans called their Japanese foundation *Mugenzai No Sono,* the Garden of the Immaculate. When he saw to its building in the early 1930s, Father Kolbe was criticized for building it on the side of a hill away from the central part of the city. However, in 1945, when the atomic bomb was dropped on Nagasaki, the Garden of the Immaculate survived with a few broken windows, while the rest of the city was nearly destroyed.

Immediately following the bombing, the city swarmed with frightened and abandoned children. The friars accepted as many of these tiny victims of war as they could into the Garden of the Immaculate. Soon an orphanage was established and in time contained 1000 children. A hero of the time and the years to come was Brother Zeno, one of Father Kolbe's original companions on the mission to Japan. Brother Zeno became widely known and loved throughout the postwar nation.

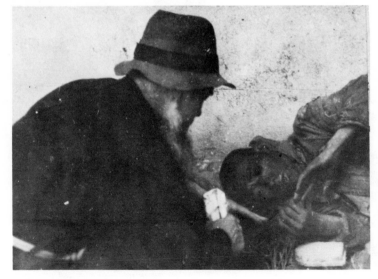

Brother Zeno, one of the original missioners to Japan with Father Kolbe, ministers to a bomb victim at the end of World War II.

6 Return to Niepokalanow

His superiors summoned Father Maximilian to Poland for the 1936 general meeting of their community. Kolbe returned to his native land, delighted with the progress in Japan, hopeful of establishing a similar operation in India, and happy to revisit the City of the Immaculate in his beloved Niepokalanow.

All, however, was not well. Father Maximilian's physical disabilities were mounting. His health had taken an inevitable downward course. Frequent hemorrhaging and discharges of blood indicated a dangerous condition.

Because of his health, his provincial superiors insisted that Father Kolbe remain in Poland at the City of the Immaculate. He willingly accepted this assignment. The friars there looked to him for the spiritual leadership they had so sorely missed during his years in Japan. They delighted in calling him father. He would respond: "I am your father, even more so than your earthly father from whom you have received your physical life. Through me, you have received a spiritual life, and this is a divine life; through me, you have received your religious vocation, which is more than physical life." To this day, men who knew him recall his spirit of intense kindness, gentleness and paternal love.

Despite his poor health and the demands of

The basilica at Niepokalanow viewed from the west.

Niepokalanow, he continued to plan and expand the scope of the Militia of the Immaculate. Several times he traveled to Italy to strengthen and support the Militia there and traveled around eastern Europe planning future Cities of the Immaculate.

In December 1938, he put Radio Niepokalanow on the air, and around that time began to make plans for an airport at the City of the Immaculate, even sending several brothers off to Warsaw for pilot training. In the late 1930s, long before the potential and the impact of television was even dreamed of, Father Kolbe was making plans to use the future medium for evangelization.

The use of mass media was the key to his ministry. Though he preached a spirituality focused on the Eucharist and on Mary, he also preached love and concern for the poor. His ministry embraced all peoples. He wrote to his followers:

> The Knight of the Immaculate does not confine his
> heart to himself, nor to his family, relatives,
> neighbors, friends or countrymen, but embraces the
> whole world, each and every soul, because, without
> exception, they have all been redeemed by the blood
> of Jesus. They are all our brothers. He desires true
> happiness for everyone, enlightenment in faith,
> cleansing from sin, inflaming of their hearts with love
> towards God and love towards neighbor, without
> restriction.

During his final years at Niepokalanow Father Kolbe was well aware of the approaching evil. ''Persecutions and wars will come," he predicted. "And when war arrives this community will disperse. That should not worry you, however, rather you should bravely comply with the will of the Immaculate."

He believed that the last stage of life was suffering and that the sooner the soul approached sanctification, the sooner the suffering would arrive. He saw this as "suffering willed through love."

One quiet evening, while sitting with a group of friars after dinner, he said: "My dear sons, if only you knew how happy I am. My heart is overflowing with happiness and peace. At the bottom of my heart an unspeakable calm reigns." He continued: "My dear sons, love the Immaculate. Love her and she will make you happy. Trust her without limits. Not all can

The gift of a new bicycle from the seminarians, sometime in the mid- to late '30s.

understand Mary. This understanding can be gained
only by prayer.'' Then the priest paused and haltingly
added: ''I have something else to tell you, but perhaps
this is enough.''

The friars pressed him to go on. ''All right, I will
tell you. The reason that I am very happy and filled
with joy is that I have been given an assurance of
heaven.''

Those who heard him make this statement
remember to this day how his voice shook. A moment
of complete silence followed. Then Father Maximilian
seemed to be ready to say something else.

The friars pressed him for more information.
Acknowledging he had received this assurance of
heaven in Japan, he continued: ''I have revealed this
secret to you to strengthen your courage and spiritual
energies for the difficulties ahead. There will be trials,
temptations and discouragements. The memory of
tonight will strengthen you and help you to persevere in
your religious life. It will strengthen you for the
sacrifice which Mary will ask of you.

''Love the Immaculate,'' he pleaded; ''love the
Immaculate.'' He begged the friars not to tell anyone
of this extraordinary conversation until after his death.
He reiterated with sorrow that only because the terrible
trial was near did he tell them of Mary's promise.

On September 1, 1939, Hitler hurled his armies
into Poland and World War II, the worst cataclysm
ever known, was launched. Within weeks German armies, superior in numbers and equipment, overran
Poland. Russians moved against Poland from the east.

Father Kolbe was under no illusions about the

treatment he would receive at Nazi hands. He had condemned in his press and on his radio station the doctrines of both Nazism and Communism. The friar frequently referred to the suffering that these godless philosophies would ultimately bring upon the world.

Furthermore Kolbe, in the last days of August 1939, spoke to his Franciscan confreres regarding his own life. He described the three stages of his life to his Franciscan brethren.

The first stage he described as a preparation for his apostolic activities; the second stage as the actual apostolate. Finally there would be the stage of suffering.

"The third stage of my life," he stated, "will be my lot shortly. It will be one of suffering. But by whom, where, how, and in what form this suffering will come, is known only to the Immaculate Mother. I would like to suffer and die in a knightly manner, even to the shedding of the last drop of my blood, to hasten the day of gaining the whole world for the Immaculate Mother of God."

The Nazis would soon oblige him.

Father Kolbe's office,
ransacked by the Nazis
in 1939.

Nazis escort Father
Kolbe and his fellow
Franciscans to prison.

7 The Final Victory

After the Nazis overran Poland, Maximilian and some of his friars at the City of the Immaculate were put into jail. It was the beginning of an overall campaign to eliminate the Polish intelligentsia, particularly the clergy.

Konrad Henlein, an assistant to the German governor of conquered Poland, explained to the Polish bishops in 1942 that "since in Poland the church and the nation are one, we must split this union. That's why we strike at once at the church and at once at the nation—to destroy you."

This first arrest did not last long. On December 8, 1939, Maximilian returned to Niepokalanow. The Nazis had occupied the place and established a concentration camp there. But they permitted Father Kolbe and a few of his friars to live there. In 1940 Maximilian actually received permission to resume printing of *The Knight.* And on December 8, 1940, he managed to publish what turned out to be the last issue of his beloved magazine.

The Gestapo, however, were watching Kolbe as a snake watches its prey. Finally they struck, and in February 1941 they arrested the priest. He was jailed just outside Warsaw, in a prison called Pawiak.

The friars prayed for his release and petitioned the Gestapo, offering 20 brothers as hostages for Father Kolbe. They were refused and told, "We must take the Poles by the head or else they will take us," a reaction to Father Kolbe's effective work in communications.

At Pawiak, Maximilian was immediately abused for his faith. While he was still wearing his Franciscan robes and a crucifix, an SS guard approached him, grabbed the crucifix and asked, "Do you still believe?"

Edward Gniadek, an eyewitness to the event, testified that Father Kolbe replied, "Yes, I do," and the guard then hit him in the face with his fist. The guard repeated the question, heard the firm reply, "Yes, I believe," and struck the priest again. The exchange was repeated until the guard gave up, stalked out of the room and slammed the door.

While at Pawiak, Maximilian was able to write occasionally to the friars at Niepokalanow, offering them encouragement and strength. "Let all brothers pray much, work conscientiously, and let them not worry, because nothing can happen without the knowledge and will of God and the Immaculate Virgin," he wrote in March. In May he emphasized this same spiritual message to the friars: "Let's permit ourselves to be guided by the Immaculate Mother wherever and however she wills it. And thus, by our faithful and conscientious service, we can contribute in winning over all souls for her."

On May 28, 1941, Father Kolbe, suffering from tubercular attacks, joined a transport of 304 prisoners to Auschwitz. There, jailers gave him identification number 16670 and first assigned him to block 17.

The new prisoners were greeted by camp commander Fritsch, who set the tone for the reign of terror that lay ahead. "You have come here, not to a sanatorium," he announced, "but to a German concentration camp from which there is just one exit, the crematory chimney. If that displeases you, you may leave at once by the high-tension wires. Now if in this transport there are Jews, they have no right to live longer than two weeks; priests, one month; others, three months.''

Nazi guards forced the seriously ill priest to haul heavy carts of gravel for the construction of the crematorium walls. Despite beatings and unbelievable indignities, the jailers were unable to break down Father Maximilian's calmness and gentleness. A fellow prisoner recalls the priest encouraging the inmates. ''No, no,'' the little friar would say, ''these Nazis will not kill our souls, since we prisoners certainly distinguish ourselves quite definitely from our tormentors; they will not be able to deprive us of the dignity of our Catholic belief. We will not give up. And when we die, then we die pure and peaceful, resigned to God in our hearts.''

A source of spiritual strength to all about him, Father Kolbe frustrated Nazi attempts to reduce these Poles and European Jews into groveling animals. Jailers reserved the dirtiest jobs for him and cursed and ridiculed him because of his priesthood. From time to time they would set dogs on him, force him to carry corpses to the crematorium, and beat him unmercifully. Eventually Maximilian collapsed with total exhaustion and was hospitalized.

Father Conrad Szweda, a fellow captive, writes:

Father Kolbe's face was lined with scars, his eyes lifeless; the fever burned in his body so that his

One of his jobs in prison was to carry the dead to the crematorium.

The crematorium at Auschwitz.

mouth dried out; he could no longer speak. But all were impressed by his manliness and the resignation with which he bore his sufferings. Often he said: "For Jesus Christ, I am prepared to suffer still more." Even though suffering intense pain, Maximilian heard the confessions of others, prayed with them, and often gave them little conferences on Mary. He was a priest every inch of his burned-out body.

By the very power of his presence, Kolbe managed to rescue these poor, beaten people from the degradation that threatened them, and somehow kept them living on a human level. Doctor Joseph Stemler, another prisoner, remembers:

Like many others, I crawled at night in the infirmary on the bare floor to the bed of Father Maximilian. The greeting was moving. We exchanged some impressions on the frightful crematorium. He encouraged me, and I confessed. Discouragement and doubt threatened to overwhelm me; but I still wanted to love. He helped me to strengthen my belief in the final victory of good. "Hatred is not creative," he whispered to me. "Our sorrow is necessary that those who live after us may be happy." His reflections on the mercy of God went straight to my heart. His words to forgive the persecutors, and to overcome evil with good, kept me from collapsing into despair.

A Protestant doctor writes of Kolbe:

. . . although tuberculosis consumed him, he remained calm . . . ; through his living belief in God and his providence, with his unshakable hope and, before all else, in his love of God and neighbor, he distinguished himself from all. Although I was in Auschwitz from 1941 until 1945, I knew of no other similar case of such heroic love of neighbor.

Despite the repeated abuse and degradation at the hands of the Nazis, Maximilian was still able to write to his mother from Auschwitz: "I am faring well. Be calm, Mother, and don't worry about me or my health. God is everywhere, who watches over all and everything with great love. It would be better not to write to me, since I don't know how long I shall remain here."

It was this indomitable man who entered the Nazi starvation bunker with nine other prisoners in July 1941.

As the prisoners marched toward the death cell they could hear the howls of torment, the curses, screams and groans of despair emanating from other starvation bunkers in the death area.

Father Maximilian walked barefoot to the underground chamber in a two-story brick building and prayed to the Virgin to whom he'd dedicated his life:

Let me praise you, O most holy Virgin!
Let me praise you at my own cost.
Let me live, work, waste away, and die for you
    alone.

Let me contribute to your exaltation, to your
    highest exaltation.
Permit that others may outdo my zeal in
    glorifying you, O Mary, so that by holy
    rivalry your glory may grow more rapidly just
    as He wills it, Who raised you above all
    creatures.
In you alone, God has been more adored than
    in all the other saints.
For you, God created the world, and for you He
    created me also.
O let me praise you, most holy Virgin Mary!

The Nazi gun butts drove the men into their death cell.
A prison guard gloated at them as they entered, "You
will come out like dried-up tulip bulbs." The heavy
wooden doors slammed shut.

But this bunker, number 11, was destined to
become like no other torture chamber in the camp. The
little priest made the difference. Gradually, under his
calm guidance and control, the men began to pray.
Although they were on the rim of hatred and despair,
the priest managed to help them sustain their faith in
God. At Father Kolbe's urging they turned to the
Blessed Mother to keep them from degenerating into
the animals the Nazis wanted them to become.

Bruno Borgowiec, an Auschwitz inmate assigned
to remove dead bodies from the death bunkers, testified
under oath:

In one bunker was Father Kolbe. The cell, with the
cold and the cement floor, had one ceiling-level win-

While at Auschwitz Father Kolbe heroically offered comfort to other prisoners.

Father Kolbe's death cell is in the basement of this building.

dow and no furniture. Just a pail for natural needs. The stench was overwhelming. Father never complained. He prayed aloud, so that his fellow prisoners could hear him in order to join him. He had the special gift of comforting everybody. When his fellow prisoners, writhing in agony, were begging for a drop of water, and in despair were screaming and cursing, Father Kolbe would calm them down, inspiring them to perseverance.

In addition to being the official undertaker at the bunker, Borgowiec was a secretary and an interpreter. After the war, as a municipal official in the Polish city of Chorzow, he recalled in detail the situation in the bunker and the death of Maximilian Kolbe:

> From the cell where these unfortunates were buried alive, you could hear the sound of prayers recited out loud, and the condemned men from other cells would join in. I had to go down once a day to accompany the guards on their inspection tour.
>
> Every time I went down there, I was greeted by fervent prayers and hymns to the holy Virgin whose sound pervaded the whole underground chamber. Father Maximilian would start them out; then everyone joined in.
>
> Sometimes they would be so absorbed in prayer that they did not even realize the guards had come for the daily inspection and had opened their cell door. Only when the SS began shouting at them would they stop praying.
>
> To give you an idea of what these prisoners went through, I need only mention that I never needed to empty the bucket in the corner (for urine).

It was always empty and dry. The prisoners actually drank its contents in order to satisfy their thirst.

Father Kolbe displayed real heroism. He asked for nothing and did not complain.

After the first week, they were so weak they had to recite their prayers in a whisper. Though the others were helplessly prone on the floor, Father Kolbe still greeted the SS inspectors while standing or kneeling among the others, a look of serenity on his face.

The guards knew he had volunteered his life in place of the prisoner who had a family. Once I heard one of them say: "This priest is a real man. I never saw one like him here before."

To the end of his long, harrowing suffering, Maximilian could amaze his captors. Indeed, the final victory was to be his. One cannot help but think of Christ emerging from his tomb to bring new life to all. Kolbe indeed in death outwitted all the evil forces of violence of World War II.

Borgowiec recalled that finally, after all but four of the prisoners had died, "the authorities decided it had gone on long enough. They needed the cell for other victims."

They ordered the camp physician, Doctor Bock, to inject the prisoners with carbolic acid. On August 14, Bock executed the remaining prisoners.

At that moment, in Cracow, it is said that a woman dressed in black fell to the street. The person who helped her up heard her say, "My son, my son."

It was Maria, Maximilian's mother. She was doing some errands and had a sudden vision in her mind

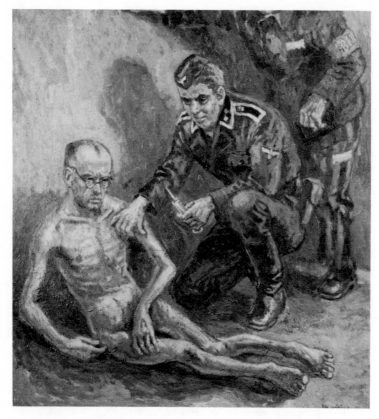

After three weeks of starvation, the Nazis killed him with an injection of carbolic acid.

in which she saw her son locked up in the death chamber. He was smiling at her, singing a hymn to the Virgin, and urging his mother to join him in the hymn.

When the guards and Bock left the starvation chamber, Borgowiec saw to his assigned task of removing the bodies to the crematorium.

In 1946 he testified:

When I was about to carry the body of Father Kolbe out of the cell, and opened the door, I noticed that he was sitting on the floor leaning against the wall, and he had his eyes open. His body was most clean and radiant. Everyone would have noticed this position and everyone would think that this was some saint. His face was bright and serene. The bodies of other prisoners I found lying on the floor, begrimed, with faces betraying signs of despair.

Before even being sent to prison, Father Kolbe had said to the friars at Niepokalanow, "I hope that after my death nothing remains of me, and that the wind blows away my dust over the whole earth."

On August 15, 1941, the feast of the Assumption of Mary, Maximilian's body was cremated at Auschwitz.

Epilogue

On October 10, 1982, Pope John Paul II presided at the canonization of St. Maximilian Kolbe, OFM Conventual. At this colorful, centuries-old ritual, the church formally acknowledged that this man who gave his life for a fellow human, was now, in the words of Cardinal Stefan Wyszynski, "seated with the princes in the kingdom of God."

For Cardinal Wyszynski, the late Primate of Poland, Kolbe had quite simply won the war. "Consider the fact," he said after Maximilian's beatification in October 1971, "that the powerful ones who had fought among themselves in this monstrous war, passed into oblivion, or into the annals of history as images of defilement and horror. Whereas the church of God drew out a forgotten man and demonstrated God's splendor before the face of peoples and nations. That is why we can boldly say that Father Maximilian Kolbe won the world war."

Though Kolbe may have been an obscure figure before the church declared him blessed, that is, worthy of veneration, he was not exactly forgotten.

One who remembered vividly was Francis Gajowniczek. He was the man who cried out for his wife and children when he was selected to die at Auschwitz; the man for whom Father Kolbe gave his life.

Several years later, in reflecting on the incident in the camp, Gajowniczek said, "At that moment it was hard for me to realize the immensity of the impression

A scene from the beatification ceremonies in 1971.

that took hold of me. I, the condemned, was to live on and someone else willingly and voluntarily offered his life for me. Was this a dream or reality? Among the companions of mutual adversity at Auschwitz there could be heard a unanimous expression of wonder at the heroic sacrifice of life of this priest for me.''

At the beatification ceremonies, Mr. Gajowniczek observed of Kolbe that ''his love for those around him was extraordinary. . . . The most splendid confirmation of his heroic love came at the end, when he offered his life for none other than me, almost a total stranger to him.''

Another who remembered well was Joseph Stemmler, a survivor of Auschwitz and a witness to Kolbe's action. Because of the debased conditions and inhuman treatment at the concentration camp, ''one

In the mid-seventies, Francis Gajowniczek, the man Father Kolbe saved at Auschwitz, visited with schoolchildren at a Franciscan community in Kenosha, Wisconsin.

man became another man's wolf,'' said Stemmler. ''In such an atmosphere came Father Kolbe's self-sacrifice. It was like a bolt of lightning in the sky or a loud thunderclap. It created a great moral shock in the prison.''

After the war the story of Kolbe's holiness and self-sacrifice soon received wider and wider notice. People began to pray to him for help and stories of his successful intercession began to accumulate. In Argentina, a person was cured of cancer; in Australia, a woman imperiled by pregnancy, had a successful delivery; in Japan, a professor was cured of a hemorrhaging wound caused by the atomic bomb explosion; in Africa, a dying monk regained his health.

The stories that grow up around such holy people contribute to the popular belief that they are with God, but such stories are not enough reason for the church to declare them sainted.

In modern times an exhaustive investigation is conducted to determine, as far as humanly possible, if the individual led an exemplary life and is with God. When reasonable human doubt is satisfied, the church then prays for miracles through the intercession of the holy person, as signs that he or she enjoys God's favor.

Though Father Kolbe died a martyr's death, a suitable reason to assume his presence with God, the church still insisted on the normal process of canonization. In 1970, two cures were officially presented and unanimously accepted by the medical and theological commissions as being beyond natural explanation—miracles.

The first involved Angela Testoni, a seamstress in

Sardinia. She suffered from tuberculosis for years, and
in 1949 was on the verge of death. The doctors agreed
that there was no hope to cure the tuberculosis that had
ravaged her lungs and intestines.

In the last year of her illness, she had begun to
pray to Father Kolbe at the suggestion of her confessor,
Father Augustine Picchedda. Both prayed more in-
tensely in the last days of her illness and she kept a picture of Father Maximilian under her pillow.

On July 24 Father Picchedda placed the picture on
her abdomen and blessed her.

"That same afternoon," she later explained, "I
felt that the abdominal pains had left me and I began to
have the assurance that I could eat without difficulty.
In fact, the following day I ate several times." In three
or four days she was able to get out of bed and by early
August was helping other residents in the sanitarium.

A number of witnesses, including three medical
doctors, confirmed the cure. In 1970, the medical and
theological commissions of the church declared that her
cure was sudden, complete, permanent and unexplainable by the laws of nature.

The other cure involved Francis Ranier of
Montegranario in Italy. He was a victim of arthritis
whose health grew worse despite treatments. He had
two amputations of parts of his right leg, but after the
operations his wounds did not heal. Infection spread
throughout his body, he lost feeling in his left hand and
became delirious. On August 4, 1949, his doctors,
acknowledging the hopelessness of his situation, said he
only had hours to live.

During the last months of his ordeal both Ranier

and his wife prayed to Father Kolbe for his intercession. They received a picture of him from a Franciscan friar, who also prayed for Kolbe's intercession. Mrs. Ranier explained that "from the very first day (of receiving the picture) we recited the prayer which was on the reverse side of the picture, and I placed it under his pillow."

Francis Ranier's son recalls that on the evening of August 4, 1949, "when we gathered together for the rosary, my mother also prayed to Father Maximilian. The picture (of Kolbe) drew my attention in a special way that evening because I was present when the picture was placed under the pillow of the sick man."

The next evening, Ranier fell even more ill, and a son-in-law, Doctor Thomas Battibocca, was summoned to give a sedative. But Francis Ranier became very calm and fell deeply asleep. When he woke up the next morning, he was cured. According to Dr. Battibocca, he was completely calm. "He understood everything, he ate his food, and he said that he felt well. His eyes were completely calm and not, as before, fixed upon one point." His daughter also related that when he woke he ate and "was completely normal." These observations were supported by several other doctors and relatives who knew Ranier's condition had been terminal.

In 1964 Ranier told the church officials investigating the cause of Maximilian that "I maintained from that time (of the cure) that I received a miracle through the intercession of the Servant of God, Maximilian Kolbe. Presently my state is normal." In 1970, the medical commission announced that the cure was

sudden, total, permanent and unexplainable by the laws of nature.

By the time of Father Kolbe's canonization, hundreds of pages of testimony had been accumulated, offering evidence of his holiness and favor with God.

Pope Paul VI declared that "his name will remain among the great," and pointed out that in his self-sacrifice Father Kolbe had fulfilled the sentence of redeeming love. Kolbe had lived up to the "secret of innocent sorrow," that Jesus has revealed: "To be expiation, to be victim, to be sacrifice, and finally to be love. 'A man can have no greater love than to lay down his life for his friends' " (Jn 15:13).

A statue captures the spirit of Maximilian Kolbe, offering the world to Mary for protection in her arms.